PLAY SMART to WIN

Better Tactics Lead to Better Results

BY

RENÉ M. VIDAL

FOREWORD BY

DICK GOULD, STANFORD UNIVERSITY

PRAISE FOR
RENÉ VIDAL AND HIS WORK

"It is difficult to meet René and not know immediately about his passion for tennis. He has done so much at different places and on different stages that it would hard NOT to gain great insight from this book. Here is a guy who has been in the trenches and has much to pass on about this game we all love."

> –Bobby Bayliss, *University of Notre Dame Head Men's Tennis Coach*

"René Vidal is the consummate professional."

> –Andy Brandi, *USTA National Coach and University of Florida Athletics Hall of Fame Inductee*

"I have known René for a number of years and have long valued his counsel. He is a trusted friend and talented executive whose own continuous growth motivates him to unlock the unlimited potentiality we all possess."

> –Keith Darcy, *Executive Director, The Ethics and Compliance Officers Association (ECOA)*

"René Vidal is a terrific coach and a true leader. We've published several articles together and collaborated on player development. Individuals and teams dedicated to performance excellence will benefit from René's expertise."

> –John Evert, *Managing Partner, Evert Tennis Academy and Former IMG Sports Agent*

"René Vidal is one of America's top coaches. His morals and ethics are above reproach. He is a 'winner' in every sense of the word."

> *–Dick Gould, John L. Hinds Director of Tennis, Stanford University (Palo Alto, CA)*

" René's book will take your tennis past - hitting and hoping. With proper execution of the strategies as outlined in Play Smart to Win, your tennis will be taken to the next level."

> *–Dave Higaki, Executive Director , East Palo Alsto Tennis & Tutoring (EPATT) Foundation*

"Throughout my junior career, René was there for me as a coach and more importantly as a friend. He helped my game grow physically and mentally as well as a competitor. René has always been there as a resource. I'm very thankful."

> *–Jesse Levine, Canadian-born American Professional Tennis Player, Career-High Singles Ranking #69*

"René is a pleasure to work with, an excellent coach. Not only did our son Matt improve on the court; off the court, Matt grew immensely as a person at a very critical stage of his life – thanks to Coach Vidal's expertise."

> *–Parents of Matthew Manasse (Purdue University)*

"We enjoy a long-standing relationship with René. By working with René, my daughter Avery significantly improved her confidence and mental game. She loved René's positive approach to coaching."

> *–Parents of Avery Wagman (USTA Nationally-Ranked Junior, Westchester County, NY)*

"It's only fitting that one of the smartest coaches in tennis writes a book on intelligent play. René Vidal's tennis insights and wisdom are timeless."

  –Paul Wardlaw, Brown University

"Caitlin enjoyed working with René because of his motivational ability. He was always looking for ways to build her up, helping her believe that she could maximize her abilities."

  –Parents of Caitlin Whoriskey (University of Tennessee All-American)

DEDICATION

Play Smart to Win is dedicated to my three sons, Angelo, Manny, and Alex, true champions both on and off the tennis court. Together, we're unstoppable.

Special thanks to author Louis Toscano for your professional editorial assistance.

TABLE OF CONTENTS

FOREWORD

By Dick Gould

What a thrill to watch the career development of René Vidal! I first met René almost 20 years ago when he served the staff of one of my summer tennis camps, while serving as Graduate Assistant to the great Greg Patton at Boise State. As I worked with René, I was instantly impressed with his desire to learn and better himself. His passion for making tennis his career was undeniable!

One of my pleasures is that we have remained in continuous contact ever since. I have proudly watched him grow professionally as a collegiate team coach, read several of his published works, and have noted his service to the USPTA and his successful Directorship of two great tennis facilities.

These varied experiences have resulted in his excellent publication of **"Play Smart to Win,"** a succinct and valuable read with four pertinent and well-organized chapters. These cover each key tactical phase of the game as it relates to style of play from singles to doubles. An important element for the reader is that almost every short paragraph is followed by bullet point summaries.

And certainly a highlight of the book is the 5th Chapter, in which René searches out answers to a series of relevant topics from tennis icons such as successful collegiate coaches Ronni Bernstein (Michigan) and Brian Boland (Virginia) and current and former USTA coaching stalwarts Jay Berger, Lynne Rolley, and Harold Solomon. This chapter is so very descriptive of René- it represents his quest to continue to learn and improve himself so as to better himself so as to better share that knowledge with others!

He has effectively done this with this very book. **"Play Smart to Win"** is a great addition to the libraries of tennis and is invaluable to both team coaches and teaching pros. It provides a vivid example of why René has become one of the most respected young personalities in tennis...

Dick Gould
The John L. Hinds
Director of Tennis
Stanford University

INTRODUCTION

The Secret To Playing Smart

"If you want to thrive, then stop doing things that are anti-thrive."

—Alan Weiss, Ph.D.

There's a story of a gentleman who sits at the helm of a multi-billion dollar industry. An astute business executive, he's become quite wealthy by dispensing timely, common-sense advice. One of his most effective solutions in reply to a client's need is to simply say *"Stop it."* A client complains about his controlling spouse, and the gentleman says, *"Stop it."* A client blames external circumstance for failure that was within her control and the gentleman says *"Stop it"*. A client threatens to jump from a ten-story building, and the gentleman says, *"Not until your check clears!"*

With over 35 years in the sport of tennis as a junior player, private and collegiate coach, director, fundraiser, and contributing author to various publications, I am certain that no game in the hemisphere lends itself to more perpetual whining, relentless alibis, overbearing parents, co-dependence (the worst of the worst), and ridiculous excuses. Don't get me wrong, I love tennis and my passion for developing leaders on and off the court is as strong as ever. In fact, that pursuit of excellence is precisely why I never allow excuse-making or negative self-talk on or off the court. In the business of sports and life, the objective is to win. Positive behaviors and habits lead to positive results. It's a straight-forward formula.

Here's the magic bullet for intelligent, winning tennis:

The secret to playing smart to win is to stop playing dumb.

Complicated? Absolutely not. One of my professional coaching mentors, Andy Brandi, likes to say, "Tennis is a simple game. We make it complicated." Amen to that. Listen, when you hit a drop shot (from 10-feet behind the baseline) that floats sky high over the net, and your opponent drills the ball through your chest, this doesn't call for thorough self-examination. *Stop hitting the drop shot.* Don't analyze your technique (you can work on this later) and certainly don't beat yourself up physically and emotionally (your opponent is already trying to do that). Just *stop* doing what you're doing and find a better tactic (choose a better shot, refocus on the next point). It's the smart thing to do.

"PLAY SMART TO WIN: *Better Tactics Lead to Better Results*" is a book about making wise decisions on the tennis court and eliminating the dumb ones. By doing the latter, you make room for the former. If you want to be successful, then stop doing things that obstruct success. Most fears are self-imposed and every failure is your responsibility to learn from, not someone else's. PLAY SMART TO WIN is an educational tool designed to help you become a more responsible, independent-minded, successful tennis player. It includes strategies and tools crafted for *your* dedicated study, *your* diligent practice, which will lead to *your* improved results. With self-discipline, genuine commitment; and mental resilience, you'll not only win more consistently, but you will truly enjoy the continual process of expanding your capabilities.

I wrote PLAY SMART TO WIN because I care deeply about high performance and view playing a role in your development as the ultimate privilege. Indeed, tennis is a tough, exciting, and ever-changing game. It literally brings champions to their knees in both victory and defeat. But honestly, would you have it any other way? I say bring the *passion*. Bring it *every single day*.

Thank you for your personal investment. To your success as you PLAY SMART TO WIN.

–René Vidal
Clayton, Missouri (2013)

PART 1

DESIGN YOUR GAME PLAN

"It's the little details that are vital. Little things make big things happen."

—John Wooden, UCLA Basketball

Design Your Game Plan

"Have a plan. Believe in the plan. Execute the plan."

—*Sylvester Croom, First African-American Head Football Coach*
in the Southeastern Conference (SEC)

A MIND TO WIN

I've heard it said that failing to prepare is preparing to fail. What this means for real competitors and higher-level tennis players is that it's your responsibility to have an organized philosophy and approach to how you will win tennis matches. Note the last three words of the previous sentence: *win tennis matches*. Not to play your opponent close, not to hope for a successful result or, even worse, praying (heaven forbid) to advance to the next round by default. When you enter the competitive arena, **the objective is to win**. There's no debate.

At every level, the top players begin with the big picture in mind (winning as the end result) by defining their own game style, based on their individual strengths and weaknesses. The very best players, the ones who have reached the upper echelons in the sport, have gone many steps further, mastering the details that have proven essential to success. To master the details is to have a plan each and every point of each and every match, each and every tournament, each and every week.

When Roger Federer steps up to the line to serve, he knows exactly where (wide, body, middle) his target is and precisely how (flat, spin, kick) he's going to get there. Before Serena Williams hits her return of serve, she's already moving forward, having decided how early she's going take the ball. Her intentions are clear. So the prerequisite to developing your game plan in preparation for battle is to channel your mindset to the dial of purpose: what you're trying to accomplish and how you're going to successfully execute. Anybody can go out and try to wing it on the tennis court. Not exactly a responsible, proactive approach. We can do better.

YOUR 5-MINUTE GAME ASSESSMENT

Developing your personal game plan for high-percentage tennis begins by having a basic understanding of:

1. **What you like to do**
2. **What you don't like to do**
3. **What you do well (strengths)**
4. **What you don't do well (weaknesses)**
5. **Fundamental tennis patterns (where, when, and how to hit specific shots)**
6. **Good decision-making (based on game style, game situations, opponents, etc.)**
7. **Court positions (attack, neutral, and defensive zones)**

"To thine own self be true", Shakespeare urged, and it's logical that the first step towards playing smarter tennis to win is attaining a heightened degree of self-awareness. The top players at every level of the sport (juniors, collegiate, adult competitive, professional) build a strategic tennis foundation that maximizes their strengths and hides or minimizes their weaknesses. In essence, they've learned what they do well, what they don't do well, and have mastered the stroke/shot patterns that provide themselves with the best possible outcomes. Champions play from and to their finely tuned individual assets. That's why they are champions. Rafael Nadal is a terrific example. When you see Nadal run beyond the deuce court towards the doubles alley to hit his forehand (avoiding having to use his backhand), it's apparent not only what his strength is, but how far he is willing to go to use his forehand to dominate opponents. Learn from the best. (And get in shape!)

The independent-minded competitive tennis player would like to believe he has created his own style of play. This is a wrong assumption. Certainly we are all unique in our abilities, but the fact of the matter is this: *there are four fundamental game styles that govern your match strategy, decision-making, shot selection, and ultimately your results.* Not even Roger Federer, a classic all-court player, or Martina Navratilova, the consummate model of the serve-and-volley method, can escape this reality.

As you engage the assessment process and further take account of your game, the following outline will help you identify where you are and where you need to go as you set out to play smarter, higher-percentage tennis:

THE FOUR FUNDAMENTAL GAME STYLES

The Counterpuncher (aka The Pusher)

- An extraordinary mover (particularly laterally)
- Has consistent groundstrokes
- Plays solid defense (passing shots, lobs, ability to slice, change pace)
- Possesses premium physical fitness level and endurance
- A fighter who psychologically never gives up
- Today's world-class professional counterpunchers include players such as Caroline Wozniacki and Novak Djokovic)

The Aggressive Baseliner

- Has at least one mighty weapon (often the forehand groundstroke)

- Is opportunistic and proactive in shot selection (looks to make something happen)
- Prefers offensive style of play as opposed to defensive style of play
- Plays a physical game based on quickness and strength
- A competitor who fully engages mentally in the battle
- Today's world-class professional aggressive baseliners include players such as Victoria Azarenka, Maria Sharapova, John Isner, and Andy Murray

The All-Court Player

- May or may not have a reliable weapon yet like to play aggressively
- Is adept at shifting between offensive and defensive play
- A master of spins and variety
- Extremely agile and typically in phenomenal physical condition
- Psychologically very flexible and adaptable
- Today's world-class professional all-court players include champions such as Serena Wlliams and Roger Federer

The Serve-and Volleyer

- Has a big, aggressive serve (well-paced as well as well-placed)
- Prefers short points, won at the net (baseline play is not a priority or strength)
- Loves to apply constant pressure and dictate the tempo of a match
- Physically owns an explosive first step and is quite agile
- A dominant, aggressive mental approach
- World-class professional serve-and-volley players include former champions such as Martina Navratilova and Stefan Edberg (Note: today's top players rarely employ this technique in large part because of the increased power of the game)

High Performance Resource #1
WORLD-CLASS DEVELOPMENTAL PLAN

PLAYER:

PLAYER GENDER/DOB/SCHOOL OR CLUB TEAM:

HEAD COACH/DEVELOPMENTAL TEAM:

<u>PLAYER EVALUATION:</u>

•

•

•

<u>PLAYER MOTIVATION (CORE REASONS WHY I PLAY):</u>

•

•

<u>LONG-TERM VISION & SHORT-TERM GOALS:</u>

<u>STRATEGY & GAME STYLE:</u>

<u>WINNING TACTICS:</u>

•

•

•

<u>TECHNICAL DEVELOPMENT:</u>

•

•

<u>MENTAL TOUGHNESS DEVELOPMENT:</u>

•

•

<u>PHYSICAL CONDITIONING DEVELOPMENT:</u>

•

•

<u>COMPETITIVE CALENDAR & SCHEDULING:</u>

PART 2

DETERMINE YOUR SHOT PATTERNS

"One must change one's tactics every ten years if one wishes to maintain one's superiority"

—Napoleon Bonaparte

DETERMINE YOUR
SHOT PATTERNS

*"High-percentage tennis is a combination of making good
decisions, based upon playing the correct shot given the ball
that's being fed to you, given your court position, your game
style, and your capabilities."*

—*Jay Berger, USTA Player Development Director of Men's Tennis*

Before you decide upon the best shots to use to maximize your game
style, it's critical to understand the importance of court coverage.
It's always preferable (in life, business, and/or sport) to take the
fastest, most effective route to your most valuable destination. I
call this the principle of acceleration. Great tennis competitors
perfectly exemplify the benefits of speed and focus. For example,
if you pay attention to the top men's professional players on the
tour, you'll learn quickly that they are all exceptional movers on
the court. These dynamos include Roger Federer, Novak Djokovic,
Rafael Nadal, Andy Murray, David Ferrer, and many more. Their
wise choice of shot is maximized by their incredible ability to cover
the court both efficiently and effectively. The premier players on
the women's professional tour are no different. Champions like
Serena Williams, Venus Williams (with her long strides), Victoria

Azarenka and others all can motor around the court with amazing anticipation, dynamic balance, and the clarity of mind to execute well under pressure.

Therefore, before building your strength-based shot patterns for better decision-making into your developmental plan, you want to understand (and consequently "own") the following keys to better court coverage. Then work on each one to improve your tennis performance.

5 KEYS TO IMPROVED COURT COVERAGE

When you improve your court coverage, you improve the number of options you have as you prepare to strike the ball. Here are 5 keys to improving your ability to move well on the court:

#1 Learn how to anticipate better.

Just as Steve Jobs and Apple anticipated the needs and wants of consumers worldwide, your responsibility is to better know what your opponent is likely to do with the ball that you've just hit. This skill will improve with time and experience. Pay attention and be alert to every detail (e.g., angle of the racket during preparation phase) that your opponent provides for your benefit.

#2 Learn how to recovery quicker.

As I coach my players and clients, *"Hit and move, don't hit and mull."* After you've hit your shot, your primary goal is to move rapidly to your Ideal Recovery Position (IRP). Your IRP will vary according to the location from where you've hit your shot, where the ball is headed, and your opponent's options.

#3 Learn your opponent's tendencies.

By understanding what your opponent is likely to do in certain situations, you will certainly upgrade your court coverage IQ. For example, if your opponent tends to hit every passing shot crosscourt, then you can approach crosscourt or down-the-line and know exactly where you should be positioned to knock off the volley.

#4 Learn basic time management skills.

Successful players understand how to manage time on the court. They recognize when they need to buy time for themselves. In this scenario, they may hit a lob to provide ample time to recover for the next shot or simply play with more net clearance. Serious players also know how to take time away from their opponents. In this scenario, a player who recognizes his opponent is off the court and out of position will look to move forward and take the next ball out of the air with a swinging volley, high volley, easy put-away volley at the net, or a well-placed overhead to finish the point.

#5 Learn the geometry of the court.

Tennis is a game of angles and options that demands all kinds of mental and physical agility, but you don't have to be a mathematician to upgrade your anticipation skills. Think of hitting your shots to locations that minimize the amount of recovery steps you need to take for the next shot. When you do this, you're *moving in the right direction.* [For a detailed analysis of court geometry, read *Think to Win* by former ATP touring professional and Pepperdine coach Allen Fox.]

> *"Time had taught me to confine my worries to the affected stroke and concentrate as usual on other parts of my game."*
> —*Allen Fox, Ph.D., and Author, Think to Win*

THE 10 COMMANDMENTS OF SAVVY SHOT-MAKING

"The ten commandments were not a suggestion."

—*Pat Riley, President, Miami Heat*

The choices you make on the tennis court are ultimately your responsibility. Just as Tom Brady is a championship football star largely because he minimizes his mistakes (makes smart decisions), you too will advance to the next level by cutting down on unforced errors and making wise choices in your shot selection. The following 10 commandments will help you reach the promised land and enjoy the view:

1. **Thou shalt first assess the match-ups.** Most players think of tennis match-ups in very simplistic terms: the opponent, a few strengths here, a few weaknesses there. I encourage you to get specific. Ask questions such as: How does my forehand match-up against his forehand? How does my backhand match-up against her backhand? How does my second-serve match up against his return? Surely Providence resides in the details. For starters, think of pre-match scouting and the pre-match warm-up as excellent assessment opportunities.

2. **Thou shalt maximize your finest strengths.** If your forehand is greater than your opponent's forehand, then seek to engage in forehand-to-forehand combat. Look to dictate points with your forehand by using not only the cross-court pattern, but the inside-out pattern, as well as the inside-in forehand pattern. The key is to identify what you do better than your opponent and then choose your patterns based on the facts. Who's controlling who?

3. **Thou shalt play within your limitations.** Players that consistently underachieve have what's called the "fantasy disease." They want to make believe that their weaker tennis strokes don't exist. As a result, they tend to overplay shots, make "dreamy" decisions, and pay the price in the win-loss column. On the other hand, the road to better shot selection is paved with consistency, playing from strength, higher net margins, larger target areas, and an ego that is

healthy and clear-sighted rather than out of control and guarantees failure.

4. **Thou shalt play to your opponent's weaknesses.** The iron-clad rule here is: choose effectiveness over expediency. If an opponent has an apparent weakness on the backhand return of serve (e.g., weak, high replies), the effective baseline competitor will adjust his game plan (selectively using the serve-and-volley pattern to the weak area, pounding the weakness). Regardless of your preferences as a player, it's your responsibility to find the weakness and work the weakness, over and over again. Not only does this work (effective), but you will often win in short order (expedience). Bottom line: if it works, continue to do it.

5. **Thou shalt consistently apply pressure.** Tough competitors practice the law of applied pressure. They've developed the instinct and ability to place their opponents in uncomfortable positions, often tempting adversaries to go for low-percentage shots. An example includes opting for a slice approach shot that stays extremely low, forcing your opponent to come up with a great shot. When would you use this pattern? In pressure situations!

6. **Thou shalt master the flow of points.** When you set up to hit a shot, you're in one of three modes: offensive, neutral, or defensive. Average players don't know which mode they're in. Better-than-average players know the mode, yet aren't fully committed to it. Great players know the mode and play the mode, every time out. It's been said that "unsuccessful people only do occasionally what successful people do daily." Once you've learned the three modes, discipline yourself to make the best choice given your position and circumstance.

7. **Thou shalt stick to "vanilla" execution.** "Flash sells tickets, boring wins matches," my friend and international tennis

expert Andy Brandi likes to say. How many times have you seen a player go for a low-percentage shot from an offensive position when a much simpler option was available? This is called "ESPN tennis." Everybody wants to have a "Sportscenter moment." But success is much more than a momentary phenomenon. Serious competitors play to execute; they don't play to the crowd. Winning matches sells tickets, save the flash for other venues.

8. **Thou shalt recognize and thrive on challenges.** An aside: In a set against Kenyon College coach Scott Thielke, after losing my service game, I proceeded to drop the next game in what had to be world-record time. Scott's words for me after the match were far from complimentary and were further exacerbated when I realized that in his victory he had lost weight (good for him) while I lost confidence (not good for me). In competition, you have to see minor and major setbacks as challenges, not threats; and see momentum changes as opportunities for resilience, not opportunities to hide in a cave. Besides, you can't hide on a tennis court but you can certainly embarrass yourself when you don't put up a great fight.

9. **Thou shalt play to your tennis personality.** Playing someone else's game will not help you win. And just because Roger Federer has found 25 different ways to hit his trademark one-handed backhand doesn't mean you should follow suit. Every player is bent a certain way when it comes to on-court style and preferences. At the same time, you don't want to fall into a mentality of "my way or the highway." The best players (and this is a quality that's worth emulating) are highly adaptable. Finding a way to win (staying open mentally) and remaining true to your strengths (staying open physically) are inextricably linked.

10. **Thou shalt learn to finish and finish well.** In this day and age, as a player, you must be able to come forward into the

court and finish points. At the recreational level, there are counterpunching players who rely strictly on defensive play and thrive. However, at every other level from junior competitive to the professional ranks, it's usually the aggressive baseliners, all-court players, and proficient volleyers that produce the best results over time. Obeying this commandment dictates that you opt for shots that successfully end points in your favor, sooner rather than later. A scenario would be when you follow-up your approach shot with a volley as opposed to retreating to the baseline (where the point re-starts all over again). All of the above requires a commitment to stretch your personal limits, expand your comfort zone, and employ prudent risk.

DOMINATE YOUR SERVE, DOMINATE THE MATCH

It's no secret that the effectiveness of your serve plays a huge role in the amount of success you'll experience as a player. This was certainly true for German-born men's professional tennis player Michael Stich. The 1991 Wimbledon singles champion credits much of his success to dominating play with his powerful serve. Just ask Stefan Edberg, whom Stich defeated in the semi-finals, and Boris Becker (finalist), both of whom are hall-of-fame professional inductees. Indeed, when we're serving well, all seems to be grand in our tennis world. Let's take a look at some of the fundamental goals and tactics that form the foundation for dictating play with your serve and notching up more wins:

Serving Goals

- The ideal objective is to serve so well as to elicit NO RESPONSE from your opponent. Pete Sampras serves as a perfect example of a champion who could ace his opponents virtually at will, regardless of whether he was up in the score or playing from behind. Sampras DOMINATED THE MATCH with his serve.
- A worthy objective is to serve so well as to elicit a SOFT RESPONSE from your opponent. Weak responses off of

your opponent's return will allow you to play on your own terms with aggressive, "offense" tennis. CONTROL THE POINT, CONTROL THE MATCH.

- The general rule of "70% first serves in" is beneficial, but perhaps not for reasons you may think. Understand that simply getting a high-percentage of first serves in play does not guarantee that you will win the point. The great benefit of high-percentage first serves is what it does for your psyche. There's a natural confidence that flows in your direction when you are hitting and placing your first serves with precision. It also alleviates the mental stress so often associated with second serves.

- The ultimate goal is to start the points on the offensive. Even if you are hitting your second serve, it's possible that with the proper amount of spin and take-off at the bounce, you can make it very difficult for your opponent to start the point favorably. Top players have an offense-minded orientation.

10 Key Tactics for Great Servers

1. Develop spin, which as my friend Allen Fox says, *"is valuable on the first serve, essential on the second."*
2. Relax. Bounce around on your toes a few times before lining up for position. The less tension in your body (and your mind), the more likely you'll be able to hit your target.
3. Proceed through your routine without deviation. Whatever works for you (e.g., bouncing the ball 3 times before pausing to serve), do it religiously. And don't worry about what your opponent thinks. Take your time (within the rules) and follow your routine.
4. Think like a baseball pitcher. Mix up your serve pace and locations to keep your opponent from a getting a good swing at the ball.
5. Visualize your serving target.

6. Always expect the return to come back in play. By being ready mentally, you'll be ready physically (on your toes, anticipation, quick first step, etc.).
7. Have a two-shot plan (see the next three keys) and play each point diligently.
8. Serve out wide to pull your opponent off the court, then hit to the open court or as a change-up behind them.
9. Serve into your opponent's body to elicit returns that land in the middle of your court. By doing this, you will control the center of the court, which leads to controlling the points.
10. Serve down the tee (over the lowest part of the net) to increase your service percentage and pull your opponent out of his or her comfort zone. Because it's difficult to create sharp angles from the middle of the court, you again will have the opportunity to control the center of the court and keep your opponent off balance and on defense.

Service Return Strategy

Henry Ford once said, "The competitor to be feared is one who never bothers about you at all, but goes on making his own business better all the time." As a tennis competitor who is preparing to return serve, your first order of business is to make your opponent play. Underachieving tennis players tend to be bothered by with the server rather than simply focusing on the ball. Home in the ball and you will increase your return percentages as well as make your opponent have to work extremely hard just to hold serve. In a recent conversation, University of Virginia head men's tennis coach Brian Boland told me he was adamant about his players striving to make 80 percent of their returns, in both singles and doubles. How do you accomplish such an extraordinary achievement? Well, first you go back to what Ford says about focusing on your own performance as opposed to becoming overly concerned with what your opponent may or may not do. Of course, top competitors will lock in on the strengths and weaknesses of their opponents – it's a process called due diligence – but the very best players focus on other variables within their control to produce high performance.

> **"THE BETTER PLAYERS ALWAYS PICK UP ON EVERY DETAIL."**
> **—Brian Boland, University of Virginia Head Men's Tennis Coach**

The following mental and tactical keys will help you take care of business as you step up to the line to return serve:

- Choose your Ideal Return Position (IRP) which tends to vary according to your strengths, your weaknesses, the speed of the serve, the location of the serve, and the spin of the serve. You can tweak this during the course of the match.

- Choose and visualize your target (e.g., return crosscourt) before your opponent begins the service motion.

- Have the appropriate blend of mental awareness (e.g., facial expressions) and physical energy (e.g., on your toes)–calm, not stressed; relaxed, not tight.

- Focus on the ball as your opponent begins the service motion, and follow the ball until you make contact.

- Take mental (or journal) notes of your opponent's serving patterns and tendencies. This includes where your opponent stands to serve, various toss locations, the different speeds and spins, and how your opponent likes to serve on key points (e.g., 30-30, ad-in, ad-out).

- Make adjustments in your starting position and shot selection based on what your opponent is showing you. For example, on a weaker second serve, you would want to start in a little closer and be aggressive with your return to dictate the point from the outset. Against a fast and powerful first serve, you want to move as far back as possible to manage the pace while not giving up too much court angle to your opponent.

HAPPY RETURNS: A DIRECTIVE FROM COACH (GENERAL) GREG PATTON

I was watching a collegiate match with the dynamic Greg Patton of UC-Irvine and Boise State fame. As one of his leading nationally-ranked players was dumping return after return in the net, Greg said, "He's not competing." The lesson was simple: the higher your return percentage, the higher your competitive level. You have to give yourself (and your team) a chance to win, and that starts by giving your opponent a chance to miss! Get the return back in play.

As you improve and develop your return game, there are a few other things to consider. Beyond getting your return consistently back in play (a form of positive applied pressure), you ideally want to start the point from a neutral position at the very least. This means that you are not scurrying around the court frantically after you put the return in play. It's a bonus to take the offense (e.g., hurting your opponent) right away off the return, but the more realistic and achievable goal is to place your return in a location that neutralizes your opponent's ability to take big swings (unless low-percentage) and allows you to set up properly balanced for the next shot on even terms with your opponent. Returning to the weaker side, adjusting court position to receive serve, and aiming the return deep down the middle are some of the best ways to neutralize your opponent's service games.

SPECIALTY SHOTS

"If you can't explain it simply, you don't know it well enough."

—*Albert Einstein, Theoretical Physicist*

Playing smart, high-percentage tennis extends well beyond your serve, service return, and groundstrokes. The following rules will

21

help you improve key and vital specialty shots such as the approach shot, volley, overhead, drop shot, and lob.

Approach Shot Rules

- **Emphasize placement, not power.** There is no bonus for speed of shot. Each point counst the same. The purpose of the approach shot is to set yourself up for good volleying position and execution.
- **Mentally relax as you move through the shot.** "Rushing" is the most common approach shot mistake that leads to poor execution.
- **Approach down-the-line.** Particularly to your opponent's weakness and/or when your contact point is above the level of the net.
- **Approach cross-court.** Particularly if you're in favorable position to hit it with force (to overcome your being temporarily out-of-position), playing the weaker side, and/or your contact point is below the level of the net. Note: if your contact point is above the net, you also have more options.
- **Approach behind your opponent.** By wrong-footing your opponent, you increase your chances of winning the point by an error or by eliciting a weak reply and putting the volley away with ease.
- **Play conservatively on low short balls that are below the level of the net.** Use slice for safety and to keep the ball low, or use mild topspin to lift the ball over the net. Be aware that excessive topspin will provide time for your opponent to effectively set up for the passing shot. Too much topspin applied to low balls also facilitates "framing" and "shanking" unforced errors. Play smart.

Volley Rules

- **Practice the right way.** It's quite rare in a match to hit a volley while standing still. The majority of your volleys are hit on the move, during transition. You'll find yourself moving forward, moving laterally, and sometimes even moving laterally *and* backwards (don't try this at home) to hit a volley. Incorporate movement into your volley practice.

- **Value position over power.** Effective volleys are all about court position: where you are on the court (e.g., close to the net, on the service line) when you're making contact (and choosing direction). Your court position determines your shot selection – or at least it should!

- **As a general rule, follow the "deep-to-deep" and "short-to-short" philosophy.** If you are closer to the service line on your half of the court, aim your volley deep past your opponent's service line. If you are within a few feet of the net, look to angle your volley off the court. These decisions will become automatic with deliberate practice.

- **Increase your intensity.** The closer you get to the net, the better your chances of hitting a winning volley. As you transition to the net, your mindset needs to be one of finishing the point, not of exploration. Don't meander. Close the net, finish the point.

- **Don't obsess over the lob.** Too many players are overly concerned about a shot that their opponent has yet to prove to utilize effectively. It's like the roller-coaster at Disney World. If you obsess about the fear and dwell upon whether to get on or not, you'll never go for the ride. Either go to the net or stay back. And make sure your opponent can actually lob first before you self-impose limitations.

Overhead Rules

- **Prepare early.** The keys to excellent overheads are more technical and psychological than tactical. Prepare your racket early and move your feet to line up behind the ball (think of an outfielder in baseball as you get behind the ball).

- **Pick a side.** Determine as early as possible which half of the court you plan to direct your overhead. Down the middle (in your opponent's direction) can be an effective third option.

- **Recover quickly.** Hitting the overhead doesn't equate to "game over." Although the objective is to win the point outright, assuming you're in an offensive overhead position, always expect the ball to come back. It's simply good psychology. Get ready for the next shot even if there is none.
- **Be prepared to hit several overheads to win.** If you watch the pros, you'll notice that even at the top level of the game, players often have to hit 3 or more overheads to win the point. Why? Good defense. Great anticipation. And yes, some mental nervousness. Keep that last point in mind when your opponent is at the net and run down that next ball.
- **Don't tie your ego to the result.** Is the overhead a difficult shot to make under pressure? Yes, it can be. But if you think along those lines, you're just setting yourself up for "shank-city." Even the pros fall for this line of thinking. Follow the fundamentals listed above, do your best, and go home without the mental baggage.

Drop Shot Rules

- **Use strategically to manage momentum.** Drop shots can provide you with both a mental and physical edge over your opponent. Not only should you technically practice this shot, but it's imperative you learn to develop your intuition to employ the drop shot at the right moments in a match.
- **Use disguise.** This takes practice. Your opponents should never see it coming, and if they do, make sure it's too late for them to do anything about it. Understand court position, yours, as well as your opponent's.
- **Hit it while inside, not outside the baseline.** Short balls provide you with the best opportunity to hit a great drop shot. Not only does your shot travel a shorter distance, but you will be in position to recover quicker for the next ball – if necessary.
- **Don't use it out of desperation.** The drop shot is a "specialty shot." Pressure points and "desperate" measures call for fundamentals, not higher risk plays like the drop shot.

24

Do not bail by allowing your nerves to get the best of you. We all want to win a match as quickly as possible, but it takes good decisions and patience for that to happen.

- **Follow up your drop shot with a lob and advance forward.** Look to follow in your lob to the net in order to finish off the point. Don't revel so much in the fact that your opponent is on a string. Finish what you start.

- **Practice your drop shot periodically.** If you can hit your drop shot where the ball lands just over the net with enough backspin to deaden the ball, you've just hit a winner. Have your professional feed you balls where you gain more points each time your drop shot bounces inside your opponents' service box.

Lob Rules

- **Put your opponent on alert.** A lob can make your opponent think twice about swarming the net. As an additional bonus, your passing shot lanes will open for you and make it simpler to successfully defend against the net-rusher.

- **Make the high defensive lob your best friend.** Not only does this make it difficult for your opponent to accurately time the overhead, but the high lob buys you time as you recover for the next shot.

- **Disguise your offensive lob.** Because most passing shots and virtually all offensive lobs are hit with topspin, it's critical that you learn to mask your offensive lob to keep your opponent guessing.

- **Play defensively when you're out of position.** Avoid the temptation to "hit your way" out of trouble when you're on your heels. Most often, a high deep return will suffice as you commit to bring the point back to neutral.

- **Keep going to the well.** If the lob is working for you, then by all means continue to use it. This isn't about sportsmanship or gamesmanship, it's about valid tactics that help win more matches.

PATTERNS: A PERSONAL STORY

Years ago, I worked for the Orange Bowl International Junior International Championships, directed by a terrific leader named Donna Fales. I remember two things from the experience: first, I didn't get paid (I served as a volunteer), and second, Donna once described to me how tennis is a game of patterns. The word "pattern" has been defined as a combination of qualities, acts, and tendencies. Thus, imagine the game of tennis as a combination of your skill sets (technical, mental, etc.), your decision-making ability (the shots you choose), and your habits (what you consistently do under pressure). Of course, your opponent will eventually enter the picture, but the better players focus on controlling their own destiny by best maximizing their unique assets. How can you effectively play to your strengths and position yourself to win every single match?

High Performance Resource #2

TOP 20 PATTERNS FOR SMARTER TENNIS IQ

How to Use this Resource

- Recognize the shot patterns and tactical options that best serve your game style.
- Diligently incorporate these patterns in both practice and competition until they become automatic.

For the Counterpuncher:

1. **After the serve or return, begin rallies by hitting the ball deep crosscourt.** Crosscourt over the lower part of the net is basic high-percentage tennis.
2. **Develop a one-handed backhand slice in addition to your topspin option.** This helps you defend the court more effectively.
3. **Rally crosscourt until you get a short ball, then drive or slice the short ball down the line or behind your opponent.** You must still be able to attack your opponent periodically.
4. **Hit high, looping topspin balls to your opponent's backhand.** You, the feisty counterpuncher, earn your fees by frustrating your opponent; this tactic will do the trick.
5. **Master the two-shot pass technique (make opponent play first volley, then go for the passing shot) and the high offensive lob.** You will speed by the competition by paying attention to these offensive and defensive tactics in your training sessions and match play.

For the Aggressive Baseliner:

6. **Practice serving to the following targets: out wide, into the body (center of service box), and down the 'T.'** Having the

ability to mix up your serves and open up the court increases your effectiveness.

7. **Develop your backhand down-the-line [drive, topspin, or slice.]** By doing so, you improve your chances of hitting a forehand on the next stroke as your opponent is likely to play crosscourt. You also wrong-foot your opponent.

8. **Use your forehand to attack your opponent's weak, shallow serve.** By taking control of the point early, you increase your winning percentages. You also shorten the points.

9. **Improve your fitness level to maximize your ability to run around your backhand to hit big forehands.** With additional speed and endurance, you can use your weapon 60-70 percent of the time. Unless you're Rafael Nadal – then it's 90 percent!

10. **Mix up your approach shots by hitting down the middle.** This tactic reduces your opponent's angle and forces your opponent to be more creative on the passing shot attempt.

For the All-Court Player:

11. **Have patience during the learning process.** Because of the wide range of skills needed to play this style effectively, it often takes the longest to develop.

12. **Invest your time practicing various shots from both the forecourt and the backcourt.** You want to facilitate the ease by which you can go from defense to offense and vice versa.

13. **Develop your swinging volley.** Made popular in the 1980's, this stroke will enable you to transition forward in the court and take advantage of your opponent's high, soft returns.

14. **When volleying a low ball, keep your shot in front of you rather than changing direction.** Playing the ball straight ahead protects your court position and reduces your chance for error.

15. **Strategically employ the drop shot when you have favorable (inside the baseline) court position.** This plays to your many talents and wears out your opponent both physically and mentally.

For the Serve-and-Volleyer:

16. **Develop a reliable second serve.** Strong baseline players and fellow net lovers look for every opportunity to exploit this area.

17. **Hit your first serve wide and volley to the open court or behind your opponent.** Known as the can opener, this is an excellent tactic to open up the court for yourself and force your opponent out of the comfort zone. This tactic to the ad-side proved to be the bane of my existence in junior tennis.

18. **Serve the weakness, volley to the weakness.** An all-out assault on your opponent's most vulnerable side provides you with the mental edge necessary to win.

19. **Kick your serve into your opponent's weakness and follow it in.** The high bounce of your serve will force a weak return, setting you up for a routine put-away volley.

20. **Chip your backhand return to the opponent's weak side and approach the net.** By taking the ball early and keeping your slice low, you apply tremendous pressure on your opponent.

My top three favorite patterns are:

1.
2.
3.

The three patterns that I plan to improve are:

1.
2.
3.

Personal Player
Signature:_____
Date:_____

PART 3

DEPLOY YOUR SINGLES TACTICS

"Give me a lever long enough and a fulcrum on which to place it, and I shall move the world."

—Archimedes

Deploy Your Singles Tactics

HOW TO BEAT A PUSHER

"It is no use saying, 'We are doing our best.' You have got to succeed in doing what is necessary."

—*Winston Churchill*

A true pusher (counterpuncher) is content to play consistently from the backcourt while waiting for his or her opponent to miss, start blaming outside forces, or commit hari kari. More often than not, the frustrated opponent falls victim to all three failing responses! It's not a pretty sight. That being said, pushers get a bad rap, but it shouldn't be this way. In fact, the "base game" of some of the finest professional champions on tour (today and in years' past) can be classified under the surprisingly auspicious style of *pusher/counterpuncher*. Look at the tale of the tape and results:

- Lleyton Hewitt   2 Grand Slam Singles Titles   Prize Money: $19.4m
- Martina Hingis   5 Grand Slam Singles Titles   Prize Money: $20.1m

- Mats Wilander   7 Grand Slam   Prize Money:
                                   Singles Titles $7.9m

I make no excuse for also placing current tennis rock star Novak Djokovic in the same class of annoying pushers and counterpunchers. Djokovic rarely misses, period. And he's been known to keep his opponents out on the court as long as possible, another mental edge strategy of the finest counterpunchers. Oh, and career earnings? *Over $48 million* at the time of this writing.

Skeptics and non-believers often question whether these types of crafty competitors are even beatable. Here's the simple truth: everyone has a few losses in them. It's up to you to make it happen by finding and exploiting the weakness. Here's what you *can do* and *need to do* to achieve winning results against ultimate pushers and counterpunchers who make the tennis world seem like a dark, scary place:

Your "Stop Doing" List

1. **Stop getting impatient.** That means going for too much too early in the point. When you do this "over and over" again, it becomes a negative pattern that results in "game over" or "end of story" for you.
2. **Stop losing it mentally.** That means focusing on the obvious fact that you're playing a pusher, then verbalizing it to anyone who's watching, who's in earshot, or to anyone who may care (they usually don't.)
3. **Stop doubting your own game.** That means choosing (consciously or unconsciously) to play your opponent's pushing game style rather than finding ways to maximize your individual assets.

Winning Tactics & Mindsets

- **Head into the match with a "lunch pail mindset."** Maintain this workhorse mentality by competing each and every point and staying out there as long as it takes to succeed.

- **Realize that many points will look alike and often will start over 4 or 5 times before they're over.** Winning involves working through the boredom and monotony.
- **Be patient by letting the points develop gradually.** The right opportunities will present themselves.
- **Play with "controlled conviction."** Take advantage of your opportunities when they arise. Be quick to exploit your opponent's weaknesses.
- **Stay true to your core game and fundamentals.** And understand that against counterpunchers, you must *finish points*.
- **Acknowledge that pushers love pace and generally have "great wheels."** They tend to move well laterally, but every opponent is different (e.g., some move forward and back quite well). Therefore, find the specific weaknesses of your opponent and exploit them rather than relying on general guidelines.
- **Mix up your shots.** Keep your opponent off balance with a select and timely use of drop shots, short angles, slices, deep topspin, and surprise swinging-volley attacks.

HOW TO BEAT A SERVE-AND-VOLLEY PLAYER

"No matter how great your natural talent, there is only one way to obtain and sustain confidence: your work ethic."

—*Jack Nicklaus*

Over the past quarter century, the most prolific serve-and-volley professional tennis players have included: Stefan Edberg, John McEnroe, Martina Navratilova, Jana Novotna, Patrick Rafter, and Pete Sampras. These fine champions, in their own way and particular style, successfully forced their opponents to:

➢ Feel absolutely helpless
➢ Watch them rather than "key in" on the ball

➢ Rush the swing of the racket ("Here come the errors')
➢ Make low-percentage decisions by "over-hitting" and "swinging for the fences"
➢ Become predictable in their approach and shot selection

Regardless of your competitive skill level, when you face a strong serve-and-volley player, you will be playing defense at least 50 percent of the time. Your opponent will apply pressure every single point of every single game. Just like today's top pros, you will be challenged to come up with big shots on pressure points. This contest certainly will summon every bit of confidence, every ounce of poise, while at the same time challenging your ability to consistently execute well under duress. Yet, with a commitment to fight and find a way to win, you can push your net-rushing opponent back on his heels and walk off the court the victor. Here are the top techniques to help you solve the serve-and-volley dilemma.

Vidal's Best Coaching Tactics vs. Serve-and-Volley Players

✓ **Give your opponent different looks by varying your return-of-serve ready position.** By distorting the court, you can disrupt your opponent's serve and volley timing.
✓ **Relax, or as we say in Spanish, "Calmate."** Make believe your opponent is not coming into the net and take your swings naturally.
✓ **Focus on the ball primarily, your opponent secondarily.** The common serve-and-volley trick is to entice you to become engrossed on your opponent, taking your eyes off the ball. Don't fall for it. Hone in on the ball.
✓ **Aim your return over the center net strap.** By doing so, you take the sidelines out of the mix, you hit high-percentage returns over the lowest part of the net, and you make your opponent play each point.
✓ **Aim your return towards your opponent's feet.** You want your opponent to "volley up" rather than hitting the first volley comfortably above the net.

✓ **Occasionally reduce the pace of your return.** A ball hit with little pace is often more difficult to handle than a ball hit with lots of pace.

✓ **Be like Ivan Lendl.** The former Czech No. 1 was never afraid to hit right at an opponent who happened to be at the net. Lendl didn't care if it was appropriate or not. Easy sitters should be put-away if possible around your opponent rather than through your opponent's belly button. But Lendl very effectively "planted seeds."

✓ **Incorporate the lob.** Depending on the power of your opponent's serve, you may be able to lob off of the return. However, I advise players to use the lob as part of their "two-shot pass" tactic. For example, hit through/drive your return, then lob off the second ball.

✓ **Keep hanging in there.** To paraphrase Gandhi's wise words: "First, the attacker ignores you, then the attacker laughs at you, then the attacker fights you, and then you win." Defeating the net-rusher is all about contesting each point without discouragement and to the best of your ability.

HOW TO BE A GREAT FINISHER

"The top players talk about doing the right things, competing hard, running well, having a good attitude, etc. The best players brainwash themselves into believing that those are the most important things about tennis – that the end result is not what the game is about."

—*Jay Berger, Former ATP Career-High Ranking No. 7*

In any sport, at every level, the business of finishing off your opponent can be an arduous, difficult task. It's why heavyweight boxing champions often end in "judges' decisions" and professional tennis matches go to a fifth set tiebreaker. No one is immune. After speaking with dozens of established coaches on the topic of closing out a match, the consensus is *it's a very, very tough, yet attainable task.*

One of the main reasons a player should prioritize becoming extraordinarily proficient at finishing off matches is because of the memories and consequences that tend to linger when you don't win. An aside: I'm still smarting from a string of high school losses that originated from a match where I was up 6-4, 4-1 only to drop that match in the 3rd set. Having allowed that singular defeat to become a huge psychological obstacle, I proceeded to lose the next 3 matches (that season) against this same player! A resume that includes a 22-4 singles record & Suffolk County finalist *should* read 26-0 county champion. Obviously, I haven't gotten over it. Don't let that be you.

From the pros to the junior and recreational ranks, no player is exempt from the challenge of a closing out a great competitor. The following half dozen keys however, will improve your winning percentages and build your confidence:

1. **Keep Believing.** The top players believe that they deserve to win the match. Not because of a higher ranking or name recognition, but due to all of the sweat equity they've invested in practice and preparation. **The greater your work ethic, the greater your confidence. The greater your confidence, the better your execution.**

2. **Stay Focused.** The top players are process- and execution-oriented, not outcome-directed. They remain focused on their in-between point routines, continuing to plan for how they will work the next point. As Michigan head coach Ronni Bernstein says, *"We try to play one point at a time and not focus on the score."*

3. **Don't Change.** The top players stick to their winning strategy and tactics. They know the specific plays and patterns that have been working and they religiously abide by them. Trying to change what's been working as you get closer to winning is a telling sign of nervousness. Your opponent will smell your fear. Don't go there.

4. **Stay Aggressive.** The superb closers *continue* to play to win, not play to lose. They stay aggressive by taking advantage of short balls, second serves, and so on. They understand that a wise opponent is always looking for the slightest chink in your armor, that one opening to turn the tide of a match. The champions take the match instead of waiting for their opponent to hand it to them.

5. **Expect Pushback.** The top players respect the fighting spirit in their opponents and expect last-ditch efforts and "final runs." It's rarely over until it's over and as WTA touring professional coach Lynne Rolley has noted, ***"The best players keep earning."***

6. **Don't Overthink.** The top players don't allow their minds to wander into unproductive territory. Thoughts that begin with "What if…" and "I hope…" do not serve your best interests when you're close to the finish line. By avoiding outcome-directed thinking and staying in the moment (e.g., "This point, right now…"), you free yourself physiologically so that you can execute your best stuff.

HOW TO SUCCESSFULLY DEFEND YOUR BACKHAND

"First of all, define why the backhand is weak. Then try and fix it."

—*Lynne Rolley, Director of Tennis, Berkeley Tennis Club*
& United States Federation Cup Coach

The backhand side is the bane of existence for players of all levels. It certainly was for me as a junior player and proved to be the insurmountable obstacle in the way of an undefeated varsity singles career record. The kick serve into the backhand had me climbing the fence in desperation. And when your opponent is closing the net like a starving animal, it makes for long days in survival mode. However, there is hope for all who strive to successfully counteract off their backhand side, and by no means should my limited tennis ability serve as an example or stumbling block for your better performance.

The first step to successfully defending your backhand is to stay away from some of the psychological pitfalls associated with the stroke. In his best-selling book, *Winning Ugly*, Brad Gilbert wrote: ***"By attempting a better shot than you're capable of hitting, you try to be an overachiever. Instead, you become an underachiever."***

5 Underachieving Temptations

1. **Ignoring the improvement of your backhand by refusing to work on it.** *"I wish it would just go away."*
2. **Hitting the mental panic button.** *"I can't deal with my backhand today."*
3. **Going for low-percentage shots off of your backhand.** *"I'll 'show' my opponent and save face with the spectators."*
4. **Allowing the pressure to negatively affect other parts of your game.** *"Not only is my backhand weak, but..."*
5. **Blaming your opponent for "playing smart."** *"All this player can do is hit to my backhand."* Well, duh, should they play to your strength?!

Lynne Rolley's coaching advice gets supercharged when you add the following guidelines to your developmental plan:

10 Performance Goals for Successfully Upgrading Your Backhand Stroke

1. Exhibit patience by playing within your capabilities.
2. Focus on consistency and depth to prevent attack and set up advantageous opportunities.
3. Adjust your court position. For the player with superb quickness, former touring professional Harold Solomon recommends a 75-25 split favoring your forehand side.
4. Understand when you can run around your backhand to hit your forehand. Less pace (more time for you to set up)

and less depth (more opportunity for you to move forward) are great starting points.

5. Take advantage of your opportunities. The willingness to take prudent risks is a positive sign of confidence.

6. Take charge early in the point by using your forehand return to attack second serves. Why play defense when you can play offense?

7. Don't change the trajectory of the ball. University of Virginia head men's coach Brian Boland advises, *"Balls that are dropping are hit with shape (arc), balls that arrive straight are hit through."*

8. Go for more margin.

9. Serve to targets where the return is likely to come into your forehand (e.g., wide on the deuce court if you're a right-handed player).

10. Learn and master the basic patterns necessary to protect your backhand and maximize your strengths. The most common patterns include developing the backhand slice, hitting your backhand down-the-line, and developing the "inside-out/inside-in" forehands as weapons.

HOW TO SUCCESSFULLY TURN A MATCH AROUND

"The power of your why is what motivates you through the grueling, mundane, and laborious tasks."

—*Darren Hardy, Author, The Compound Effect*

If you've ever watched Olympic figure-skating, then you're well aware of the fact that the tiniest misstep can make the difference between medaling or dropping out of contention. It doesn't take much for a performance to literally spiral out of control, taking the athlete's dreams along for the ride. We face similar challenges in tennis. For example, the match begins and before we know it, we're down two breaks of serve or we're down a set and a break. It seems as if the match is out of our control. Undesirable temptations such as speeding up the pace (to get off the court as quickly as possible), refusing to assess and/or change strategy, quickly rear their ugly heads. The best players never throw in the towel. Unlike figure skating, where the slightest mistake can be fatal, the smart tennis player believes there is still time to turn things around.

The following keys and tactics will help you keep your opponent out on the court longer and improve your chances of claiming victory from what looks like imminent defeat:

7 Techniques for True Resilience

1. **Assess what's happening strategically.** Is it your execution that's failing or do you need to change your tactics?
2. **Pick the right time to change.** If you're down a break of serve in the first set, it's probably too early to change your strategy. However, if your opponent is up a set and a break, the time for change is now. Remember that each match is different and you must be plugged in emotionally to make good decisions.
3. **Walk with a positive purpose.** Positive body language communicates that you're still playing to win, that there's hope for you. The unfavorable alternative: a downcast, low-energy, negative demeanor communicates that you don't have the confidence in yourself to turn things around. That's called game over.
4. **Seek to influence, not control your opponent's game.** Andre Agassi often talked about the need for his opponents to "feel his game." Agassi was always out to make an impression on his opponent that of course worked in his best self-interest. You can't control how well your opponent is playing, but you can certainly influence your opponent by displaying a strong mental, physical, and strategic presence. Don't just "go away." Influence and impress.
5. **Slow the tempo down.** The tendency for average players who find themselves down in the score is to quicken the

pace. This is a huge mistake. Your objective is to take as much time as you need, within the rules, to maintain your clarity, composure, and to positively influence the momentum of the match.

6. **Rely on your pre-point routines and habits.** Rituals such as walking to the back fence, adjusting your racket strings, engaging in positive self-talk, and so on are all useful methodologies for keeping your mind and body relaxed and calm. Your job is to figure out a way to get back in the match. This can only be achieved with a peaceful and quiet mind.

7. **Buckle down on each point.** At the very least, cut your unforced errors in half. This is not the time to donate points to your opponent. There's no room to be careless when you're trying to reverse the tables on your opponent. Start with first serves and high-percentage returns. Your job is to compete, and winning tennis begins with a foundation of consistency.

High Performance Resource #3
THE SEVEN LAWS OF MENTAL TOUGHNESS

"Credibility is developed and sustained by proving yourself every single day."

—Andy Brandi, Inductee, University of Florida Athletic Hall of Fame (2012 Interview with René Vidal)

THE LAW OF PREPARATION

Maximum tennis performance is preceded by intense, thorough preparation.

THE LAW OF BELIEF

The well-prepared players who truly believe they can win create their own successful realities.

THE LAW OF EXPECTATIONS

Your expectations, positive or negative, become your very own self-fulfilling prophecies.

THE LAW OF CONCENTRATION

Exclusive focus and attention to each point increases your chances of winning.

THE LAW OF EXECUTION

To consistently perform under pressure is the mark of a great champion.

THE LAW OF POISE

The self-confident competitor exudes composure at all times.

THE LAW OF RESILIENCE

Top competitors withstand and overcome challenges, difficulties, and adversity.

PART 4

DOMINATE YOUR DOUBLES OPPONENTS

"The most important thing in communication is hearing what isn't said."

—Peter Drucker

DOMINATE YOUR
DOUBLES OPPONENTS

"Teamwork is the essence of life."

—*Pat Riley*

As a junior tennis player, I didn't play much doubles. With the advent of western grips in 1980s and the rise of Bjorn Borg, I was a baseline guy. In fact, the game of doubles "taking a back seat" is still quite common in today's junior and professional ranks. Where doubles truly thrives is at the recreational level and on the collegiate circuit, where team trips are won to dreamy locales like Palm Springs, and national championship trophies hoisted as a result of outstanding team play. Personally, I competed in doubles for my college program at the # 3 position, which tends to be the home of players with weak volleys and subpar doubles IQ. I did play # 2 singles which further highlights the disparity. It wasn't until I coached doubles at the Division 1 collegiate level that I became passionate about its' science and value. Fast-paced and high-pressure college doubles provides the hyper-competitive personality an opportunity to engage in the ultimate combat with a member of one's own tribe and with a common objective. Without a doubt, it's fun stuff! At the recreational level, the stakes can be just as high for players who simply love to compete. And the stories I hear and at times witness as a coach support competitive doubles as a feisty, thrilling environment where winning is not "recreational"; it's *sport.*

AMAZING BENEFITS AND NEGATIVE TENDENCIES

Playing doubles can offer some terrific experiences. It also has several other benefits:

- ✓ It improves your volley game, helping you become a more complete player.
- ✓ It forces you to "get out of yourself" and "get into the team."
- ✓ It builds the confidence of the introvert through effective partner communication.
- ✓ It increases your shot accuracy as you often have limited options in which to hit.
- ✓ It develops your serve as you execute basic serve-and-volley patterns for success.

Before you can begin to reap the benefits of competitive doubles, there are a few obstacles (all self-imposed) that seem to be most common among players who fall short of their potential. Doubles players who find themselves consistently underachieving may want to review (and reverse any or all of) the following 5 negative tendencies:

1. A tendency to pick your partner solely based on likeability rather than factoring in emotional, strategic, and technical (strength-weakness compatibility) chemistry.
2. A tendency to want to be the "star player" rather than approaching the winning process with a team mentality.
3. A tendency to "talk down" and/or "talk less" to your partner when under pressure rather than solving problems together.
4. A tendency to want to be the "shot maker" rather than making high-percentage tennis the rule.

5. A tendency to undervalue and underutilize good, solid defensive doubles strategies, forgetting the importance of balance and doing what you need to do to influence results.

Most of these tendencies are the result of an emotional drive inadequately applied. For example, the need for attention drives a player to hog 70 percent of the court and "want the ball" even when common doubles sense says otherwise. Furthermore, a player's tendency to talk down to his partner is a reflection of emotional immaturity and insufficient interpersonal communication skills. Each of these negative emotional tendencies needs to be turned around (eliminated completely or at least "put in a corner") and transformed into positive realities. For all parties involved, the sooner the better. You never want to find yourself without solid, credible opportunities for a great partner and players two and three levels below you are not real attractive options.

25 KEYS TO UNLOCKING YOUR
TEAM'S POTENTIAL

I've always viewed doubles as more science than art. There are repeatable high-percentage tennis patterns in both singles and doubles, but you'll find that each doubles player has a specific role to play, specific responsibilities to fulfill, and has fewer overall options in terms of strategies, court position, shot selection, targets, and so on. In singles, the game and court is wide open. Also, in one-to-one combat, more elements (e.g., psychological shifts, slices, spins) come into play during a match.

My experience has overwhelmingly demonstrated that successful doubles boils down to doing a few things really, really well. Look at the following 25 keys and choose which ones will unlock your team's potential and accelerate your improvement on the court:

1. Pick the best partner for you, one who complements you in as many facets of the game as possible and whom you both enjoy and respect.

2. Take stock of your team's strengths and weaknesses as you decide who plays which side of the court.
3. Make "team success" your mantra.
4. Give the relationship time to evolve, but change it if you're consistently "seeing red flags."
5. Decide your communication frequency. More is better than less, but choose what's best for your team personality.
6. Learn the "4 Roles of a Doubles Player": Server, Server's Partner, Returner, Returner's Partner. Each role comes with specific responsibilities. For example, did you know that the server's partner bears much of the responsibility for his teammate's ability to hold service?
7. Focus on your responsibilities. Coach yourself, not your partner.
8. Body language speaks volumes. Look on the outside the way you and your partner want to feel on the inside.
9. Communicate towards winning and agreement, not personal dominance. "It seems like her backhand is weaker" is more effective than the commanding "Serve to the backhand."
10. Emphasize court position over stroke and shot production. Court position is science, not a creative pursuit. Know where you should be and position yourself properly, then focus on execution. Great question: Was I in the best position to execute?
11. Go with the flow by playing offense when on offense (e.g., at net) and playing neutral or exercising patience when on defense (e.g., at baseline).
12. Play "straight vanilla" tennis. Example: aim down the middle against two players at the net. High-percentage tennis is the rule.
13. Volley in the direction that you are moving. The alternative takes you and your partner out of position. Keep this point in mind when you're poaching.
14. Decide to poach before your partner serves. Obviously, you can instinctively poach on a weak return, but you want to be definitive and proactive. Make something positive happen.

15. Speak clearly and passionately during the point (e.g., "Mine, switch! Loud, not soft.).

16. As the server's partner, stay aggressive. The right mentality: "The key to holding serve is in my hands."

17. Expand your options by learning and practicing the varied service (e.g., Australian) and return (e.g., Two-Back) formations.

18. Strive for a first-service percentage of 75 or 80.

19. Make 80 percent of returns in play your goal. Of course, timing is everything – make your opponent play on key points such as 30-30, deuce, etc.

20. Present yourselves as a wall by owning the middle of the court.

21. Go for "sound play" over "stylish play." The best doubles teams are disciplined in their shot selection.

22. Remember, doubles is won at the net. Play effective defense when you must and look for opportunities to advance to the net (as a team).

23. Take pride in your problem-solving abilities. There's nothing you can't accomplish as a team when you work together towards a common goal.

24. Make adjustments, and then make some more. Your opponent's lob shouldn't stifle your game. Re-orient your court position, take the ball out of the air, and show no frustration. You always have favorable options.

25. Take responsibility for the results. There's no room for blaming and excuse-making in the winner's circle.

High Performance Resource #4
OWN YOUR ROLE, WIN MORE MATCHES

The Server's Role

❖ Communicate with your partner the upcoming point strategy. Coordinate poaching and use of signals.

❖ Strive for a first-service percentage of 70 percent or higher.

❖ Position yourself well for your first volley with an explosive first step.

❖ Look to move forward after your first volley.

❖ Change up your serving formations to improve and/or increase your momentum.

The Serving Partner Role

❖ Communicate with your partner the upcoming point strategy. Coordinate poaching, use of signals.

❖ Take full responsibility for poaching on every floating return. Go!

❖ Move forward on an angle, not laterally, for effective poaching.

❖ Follow the ball for excellent court positioning.

❖ Distract your opponents with efficient, constant motion while at the net.

The Receiver's Role

❖ Communicate with your partner your starting team position and point strategy. For example, you can play traditional one-up, one-back or two-back, then strategize as to where you will go after the return.

❖ Consider positioning lefties in the deuce court so that both forehands are in the middle.

❖ Strive for a return service percentage of 75 percent or higher.

❖ Watch the ball from your opponent's toss to block the poacher out of your mental picture.

❖ Aim middle over the center strap on your second shot as a general rule.

The Receiving Partner Role

❖ Communicate with your partner your starting team position and point strategy. For example, you can play traditional one-up, one-back or two-back, then strategize as to where you will go after the return.

❖ Focus your attention on the Serving Partner as the point begins.

❖ Move forward towards the net *after* your partner's return goes crosscourt.

❖ Look to poach and stay aggressive once the point begins.

❖ Don't understand the estimate the power of the two-back position – playing to win for doubles requires wisely submerging two egos.

PART 5

DEVELOP YOURSELF BY LEARNING
FROM THE BEST

"The time to raise the bar is when you're already on top."

—Alan Weiss, Ph.D.

Jay Berger

Director of Men's Tennis, USTA Player Development

ATP Career-High World Ranking #7 (1990)

Boca Raton, Florida

"The sport of tennis is about decision-making."

Vidal: How do you define high-percentage tennis?

Berger: High-percentage tennis is a combination of making good decisions, based upon playing the correct shot given the ball that's being fed to you, given your court position, your game style, and your capabilities. Ultimately, high-percentage is all about decision-making. The biggest mistake we see kids make for example: they're inside the court and they play the ball too high or when they're deep in the court, not playing with enough margin. I've also found that the inside-in forehand is a pretty abused shot; players hitting this shot while falling to the left is a huge violation of good decision-making.

Another key to high-percentage tennis is understanding time, understanding when you need time and creating that time for yourself. You accomplish this through your movement and/or the ball that you play back. Great players also intuitively understand how to take time from players. At the end of the day, I'm learning more and more that the sport of tennis is about decision-making.

Vidal: What are your top 3 coaching strategies for helping players become better decision-makers?

Berger: First, I organize their game to have them better understand what a good decision is, some of the patterns they are going to use; not giving ultimatums, simply educational. Second, I begin with racquet drilling where they're working on patterns, move to modified live ball drilling, and then to a much open style of training and playing a ton matches. Finally, I use video. It's a terrific teaching and coaching tool.

Vidal: From a strategic and tactical perspective, how has the professional tour evolved since your playing days?

Berger: Because the men's players are a lot stronger today, they're really able to hurt opponents from bigger areas of the court (e.g., balls that are 3-4 feet behind the baseline). Second, the movement of the sport has drastically improved where you have guys that are 6"4 moving as well as guys that were 5"8 back when I played. Therefore, what might look like an opening might not be a true opening. Third, physical strength has had a significant impact on the game. For example, if you come to the net, players are able to put so much torque and rotation on the ball that you really need to come in on a great shot. Thus, there are a lot less serve-and-volley players; guys are much better from the backcourt and generally everybody has a big serve and big weapons in today's pro game.

Vidal: Can you discuss the importance of playing instinctively as it relates to being a good thinker on the court?

Berger: Here at the USTA, I tell the kids every day that there are a thousand players that hit the ball well but the key is to have the instinct and the vision to select the right shot at the right time; knowing when to play a little safer, when to apply a little more pressure – understanding all of these aspects of the sport – picking up patterns, etc. The best players are so engaged on the court and have probably been like that since they were kids; the patterns that they are able to pick up are pretty extensive.

Vidal: How do you go about developing some of that instinctiveness in players that aren't quite there yet?

Berger: It begins with kids understanding what their capabilities are and what they should do with certain balls. The ability to recognize the ball is huge. The ability to foster independence in a player is also vital. What I've learned as a coach is the importance of asking questions and not always providing the answers for the player. You want to make sure you're not over-coaching. The players have to go out there and figure things out on their own during matches. On that note, playing an enormous amount of matches, point play, and live ball (drills), really helps create instincts for what actually occurs in real competition.

Vidal: In terms of strategy and tactics, what are some of the key differences you've observed among the professional ranks vs. top collegiate and junior players?

Berger: Shot selection: being able to read the ball, understanding that when you're inside the court, you're not going to miss long and when you're deep in the court, you're not going to miss in the net. It's critical that players understand that tennis is still a game of errors. If you watch the best players in the world, the winners they hit are to pretty big spots (large areas) in the court. They're not hitting lines or an inch from the line; watch Djokovic for example and you see him open up the court and he's hitting winners 4 or 5 feet inside the sidelines. On the other hand, when you watch the college players or the juniors, their shot selection is pretty suspect where the basic principles aren't really followed.

Vidal: Besides more repetitions, what's your tactical advice for players with weaker backhands?

Berger: First of all, if you have a weaker backhand, you should learn some of the basic patterns that you need to play to protect it. The next step is applying those patterns. Patterns and tactics include using your inside-out forehand a lot, using your down-the-line backhand a little bit more, and developing a slice that can neutralize players.

Vidal: When competing against a pusher or counterpuncher, are there some general tactical guidelines that players should follow?

Berger: First, you have to be more patient and selective when picking your opportunities. It's important to be more calculated with the way that you play. For example, if you're competing against a real good counterpuncher, you may want to put them in a position where they need to be the aggressor. This is all given that your base game is not better than their base game. If your base game is better than theirs, then you just beat them like that. I like to make those players (counterpunchers) come forward into the court and I'm going to be precise about the balls that I'm going to attack. A good counterpuncher is going to have you push the envelope a little more and it becomes a game of intelligent risk.

Vidal: How do you coach your players to be great finishers, to close out sets and matches on a consistent basis?

Berger: That's difficult and much of what tennis is about. It's more of a mindset. Tennis is a decision-making sport. Obviously we all want outcomes, but if you listen to all of the top players, they talk about doing the right things, competing hard, running well, having a good attitude, etc. The best players brainwash themselves into believing that those are the most important things about tennis – that the end result is not what the game is about. If you can put yourself in that mindset, great things will happen. Also, great finishers are at peace with the fact that they've done everything in their power to prepare for matches and really deserve to have a positive outcome.

Yet, finishing matches is often one of the toughest moments in tennis. When I look at the matches that I played, there are 2-3 matches that I really choked, but I still won them. The point is that you have to have an optimistic perception; it's how you deal with the choking. I also believe that the best players in the world are unbelievably optimistic. They always think something good is going to happen.

Vidal: What's your approach to scouting and how do you incorporate it into pre-match preparation?

Berger: As a player I wasn't much of a scouter. I had a lot of confidence in my ability to make decisions on the court. Of course, I wanted to know some basic things, but I think scouting can be overdone. I believe that you want to focus more on the things that you do on the court, but at the same time it's really beneficial to know what your opponent's tendencies are. Knowing for example what their favorite serve is or if they'll serve-and-volley, but I still think the game plan has to revolve around what you do on the court, unless there's just an absolute glaring weakness in your opponent. In the end however, I think scouting (today) is becoming more important with all the video available; this helps you get an idea of how guys truly play. It's also important how the coach uses that information.

Ronni Bernstein
Head Coach, Women's Tennis
University of Michigan
WTA Career-High World Ranking #30 (Doubles) & #78
(Singles)
Ann Arbor, Michigan

"The best players have a plan during each and every point."

Vidal: What does high-percentage, winning doubles look like to you?

Bernstein: Winning doubles looks like doing the basics very well. Making a high percentage of first serves, making returns and first volleys. Being aggressive and moving to the net. Here at Michigan, we place a high value on playing through the middle.

Vidal: How do you define high-percentage tennis for singles?

Bernstein: High percentage singles means keeping the ball deep and cross court. Changing direction on the right ball. Good height over the net. Limiting the unforced errors and playing smart tennis. Much depends on your opponent and their game style.

Vidal: From a strategic and tactical perspective, how has the professional tour evolved since your playing days

Bernstein: Tactically the game has changed a lot. Players were more creative and didn't hit with as much power. The equipment has changed so much that it has become a power game. Grips are different too and players generate so much more spin now. It's very tough in today's game to come to net because people hit the ball so big. The game has completely changed.

Vidal: Can you discuss the importance of playing instinctively as it relates to being a good thinker on the court?

Bernstein: Playing instinctively is reacting rather than thinking. I do think that tennis can be like a game of chess where you construct the point always thinking about the next ball. Sometimes players just bang away without any real thought about what will occur next. The best players have a plan during the point and react to the shots that they are hitting.

Vidal: In terms of strategy and tactics, what are some of the key differences you've observed among the professional ranks vs. top collegiate and junior players?

Bernstein: Strategy and tactics to me are the same no matter the level. At least, that is what I believe. College players are attempting to construct points like the professional players but just not at the same level of efficiency.

Vidal: Besides more repetitions, what's your tactical advice for players with weaker backhands?

Bernstein: My advice for weaker backhands is obviously repetition first but we would work on the non-dominant hand have more of a presence in the swing. For a righty, we may hit tons of lefty forehands so they get the feel of using that hand on the backhand side. We would also work on more spin on the ball for higher margins over the net. It really would depend on what was the cause of the backhand weakness.

Vidal: How much time should players invest on strengths development vs. improving weaknesses?

Bernstein: I think this should be 50-50. You don't want to neglect the strength because it could quickly become the weakness. We work on players strengths a lot too as it builds confidence and makes them feel better on the court.

Vidal: When competing against a pusher or counterpuncher, are there some general tactical guidelines that players should follow?

Bernstein: My phrase would be to be "patiently aggressive." You want to continue to play your game but you need to make sure you are not going for too much too soon. Smart players patiently work the point and step up when the opportunity arises. It's important to make sure that players do not fall into the pusher's game and continue to focus on their own game and how to be successful.

Vidal: How do you coach your players to be great finishers, to close out sets and matches on a consistent basis?

Bernstein: We try to have them play each point the same and not focus on the score. We talk all the time about the process and not focus on the score. Keep to the strategy and game plan and everything else will take care of itself. The biggest mistake a player can make is when they are trying to close a match out is to sit back and wait for opponent to miss. We talk about stepping up and taking some risk when trying to close out a match. We also talk about taking their time in these situations and making sure they have a plan before the point starts.

Brian Boland
Head Coach, Men's Tennis
University of Virginia
ITA National Coach of the Year (2008)
Charlottesville, Virginia

"Winning doubles is about court position."

Vidal: What does high-percentage, winning doubles look like to you?

Boland: First, 80% 1st serve percentage. When you get your first serve in, you tend to win 70-80% of the points. On the second serve, it's closer to 50%. Second, 80% return percentage. This means to get the ball back. We feel statistically, 80% always gives us a chance to break in an 8-game pro-set. And at the highest levels of the game (doubles), you're really looking for just one break. I don't think it's outrageous to ask our guys to get 80% of their returns in the court. The quality of the return at a high level is making the ball. Third, owning the middle of the court when at net. Winning doubles is about court position. If you're constantly not giving up the middle of your court and constantly using the middle of the court, you present yourselves as a wall to the opposing team. You'll rarely get beat if you don't give away the middle. I think it's a great way to look at high-percentage doubles. Fourth and finally, making disciplined decisions off the ground when serving/returning and staying back.

Vidal: How do the roles of personalities come into play when you're pairing teams together?

Boland: Good coaches can find a way to help players learn to compete effectively as a team. I've had guys that didn't particularly get along well, but because of their game styles, they were unbelievable teams. Plus they wanted to succeed, wanted to develop, so they put their egos aside and focused on doing what it takes to win. The point is that if you put a doubles team together just because the players get along, understand that it's not always going to necessarily work.

Regarding game styles, I had a player (Michael Shabaz) who won a couple of national doubles championships who played particularly well with a big guy and a big serve. He didn't really need someone who was great off the ground. Michael could rely heavily on his serve and off his groundstrokes; all he needed was a player at the net who could put the ball away. And Michael also had one of the best returns in collegiate tennis; he made over 80% of his returns – that's why he won two national championships.

Vidal: How do you define high-percentage tennis for singles?

Boland: 1) High 1st Serve %, 2) High Return % 3) DEPTH to BIG TARGETS off the ground in order to EARN opportunities to OPEN THE COURT, TRANSITION or DROP SHOT.

Vidal: When you're on the recruiting trail, what are the characteristics that get your attention and draw your interest in a player?

Boland: Someone who can defend their court first. I want to know if he is *willing* and *able* to defend his court. To defend your court, you have to be resilient, tough, and hang in points that most guys want to check out on. To me, when you're willing and able to defend your court, and defend it well, you're often times an extremely competitive person.

Then, I believe you can teach a player what he can do to step up to the line and hit through the court. So, I prefer a player who can defend their court first and then we can work from there. I look and value players who are not concerned with how it looks – they're true competitors. I love to work with guys who will compete against anyone, anytime, anyplace; they simply love to compete. They're not only committed to making their opponents extremely uncomfortable but they really work on becoming a complete player. It starts with a willingness and the ability to defend your court. Note that this doesn't mean that I believe in defense first. Like Dick Gould (Stanford), I believe you want to put as much pressure on your opponent as you can, but in today's game, you have to defend your court as well. Certainly at the highest levels of tennis, you have to be able transition and hit through the court, but first and foremost, you have to defend the court.

Vidal: From a strategic and tactical perspective, how has the professional tour evolved since your playing days?

Boland: Every player inside the top 100 ATP now has a relatively complete game in the sense that everyone serves, returns and plays off the ground extremely well. The transition game has become somewhat of a lost art in today's game but I do believe that the very top players are taking more and more balls out of the air when the opportunities arise. Today's modern game has turned into a war of movement, fitness and who can hit the biggest ball (with margin) regardless of where they are on the court. Players today are playing a little deeper behind the baseline at the start of points so they can take full swings on the ball with the purpose of earning shorter ball opportunities off their heavy shots. As a result, the players are physically stronger nowadays than they were in the 80s, 90s and early 2000s and every year the players at the very top continue to push the sport's benchmark of athleticism with how they move on the court. Because of how well players are moving is a major reason why I, and many other coaches believe, that taking balls out of the air is becoming a necessary skill to own as a world-class professional.

Vidal: Can you discuss the importance of playing instinctively as it relates to being a good thinker on the court?

Boland: I believe there are NATURAL decision-makers and TRAINED decision-makers at the very top of our sport. The natural decision-makers rely on their feel to make great decisions with their shot selection and the trained decision-makers have programmed themselves to know where, why and how every ball should be hit through millions of quality repetitions in practice and matches. At the end of the day, I believe, for the most part, that the very best players in the world play on automatic pilot as far as their shot selection goes. However, without quality practices both the natural and the trained decision-makers run the risk of playing unorganized tennis. A player's feel for the game can only take him or her so far and that is why quality WORK is necessary to be great regardless of your natural ability. Lastly, I believe most of *the best players in today's game walk on the court with specific objectives* and they are masters at making the execution of those objectives their identity rather than the result of the match.

Vidal: In terms of strategy and tactics, what are some of the key differences you've observed among the professional ranks vs. top collegiate and junior players?

Boland: 1) The professionals make less unforced errors 2) The professionals play with greater depth 3) If the ball hits the strings on the return, the pro makes it almost every time (especially on 2nd serve return) 4) The professionals panic less often during and in-between points 5) The professionals are opportunists in terms of recognizing opponent tendencies, body language, when to defend and when to attack. They play close attention to everything during a match!

Vidal: Besides more repetitions, what's your tactical advice for players with weaker backhands?

Boland: 1) For Righties, serve wide on the deuce and T (center) on the ad a lot because most of those returns will come to your forehand. For Lefties, vice versa. 2) Stating the obvious – look to hit more forehands! 3) Play more backhands down the line or middle so that you have a better shot of receiving a forehand on the next ball. 4) Keep the trajectory of your backhand simple. Hit the ball back towards the same (or similar) angle that it arrived unto your racquet. (e.g., balls that are dropping are hit with shape, balls that arrive straight are hit through the ball and balls that are rising at or above your shoulder are driven slightly downward.) This should add conviction to your backhand, which will improve acceleration and weight transfer.

Vidal: How much time should players invest on strengths development vs. improving weaknesses?

Boland: At the college and pro level, I would say for the most part 80% strength development and 20% improving weaknesses but it depends on the time of year. During the competitive phases of a year, players must learn to compete and put themselves in a position to win with what they do best but during the off-season or fall months of the college season, the scale might tip a bit more towards improving a weakness.

Vidal: When competing against a pusher or counterpuncher, are there some general tactical guidelines that players should follow?

Boland: Generally, the faster you play them, the more comfortable they feel. The more you make them run, the better they hit the ball. Lastly, the more you show them the attack, the more prepared they are to neutralize. Therefore, take your time and let the point evolve. Hit behind them a decent amount and surprise them with the attack. Especially against a counterpuncher, do not play looking for the short ball. Focus more on earning the short ball and recognizing it when it arrives. You do not need to anticipate the short ball. The short ball will appear if you work to earn it. Remember, sometimes the first or second opportunities to attack might not be the right times to go on the offense. It's all about timing when attacking a counterpuncher and when you do, do it with controlled conviction.

Vidal: How do you coach your players to be great finishers, to close out sets and matches on a consistent basis?

Boland: I try and teach them to pick a play with their serve and 1st ball or really focus on executing the type of return they want to hit off a 1st or 2nd serve. Once again, when the pressure is on, I want my guys to play on automatic pilot and have no doubts as to how or where they need to play their shots. Clearly, I encourage our players to be on the offensive from the get go if times allows, especially when serving or returning a 2nd serve and I would say that is the number one objective for finishing a match. You want the ball on your racquet, to be in control of your own destiny and have your opponent at your mercy when closing out a match. Picking plays and an offensive mentality are very helpful tips during these moments. If your player is a counter-puncher, then the mentality needs to be, "I am going to get my feet behind every ball, play as deep as I can, out work this guy and send him to the hospital, (figuratively speaking of course)." The way I communicate with my players when closing out a match (or in general) is so different according to their personalities, emotional state and my experiences with them. The way I handle these moments is such a game time decision. And sometimes, I have found that it is best to say nothing at all.

Lynne Rolley
Director of Tennis, The Berkeley Tennis Club
Inductee, Northern California Tennis Hall of Fame
Berkeley, California

"Whether it's the first point of the match or the last point of the match, you've got to earn it."

Vidal: How do you define high-percentage tennis?

Rolley: High-percentage tennis is not a reinvention. Percentage tennis means making the right shot choices and playing the proper patterns to give you a larger chance of being successful in winning points in a match. As long as you do this consistently, for most of the time, chances are you will end up winning most matches.

For great players, percentage tennis can also have a different meaning. They have different mindsets. Most often you might instruct them to execute what works well for them. For example, some people are more fragile in certain areas than others. It's all a puzzle. I spent 10 years with Lindsay Davenport; she had other coaches, but I was always her mentor because I could figure out how to keep the ship going in the right direction. It's about the relationship, the knowledge, and how to manage a player, that makes it all work. In Lindsay's case it was about building a good, solid team around her that made her play percentage tennis.

Vidal: Can you share your approach for integrating strategy and tactics into your junior player's developmental plan?

Rolley: As a coach, you get to know your player as an individual. You want to look at the qualities they have at that moment and the strengths that you think they might develop as a mature player. Number one, it's important that students like how they play, how they perceive themselves as players, the shots they like to hit and so on. Then, it's important to develop 3 or 4 patterns that are truly going to work for them. If in doing that you find there's an apparent weakness, you need to try and fix it. You also need to know how in what area your player is vulnerable. Where are they solid? Where are they great? That's how you design their game. Then teach them how to work on it so they don't try to do too many different things. Keep their game geared towards them. For example, Caroline Wozniacki doesn't play the same way as Victoria Azarenka . Serena plays differently than Radwanska. But if you were able to look at all those 4 women when they were kids, you would know that they would play that same style when they become pros. Radwanska fundamentally plays the same way now as she played when she was 14.

So the game was set, the idea, the picture of what this player was going to be was pretty well in place. They get great at what you think they can get great at. It's critical to look at what a player has and determine if he or she can go from good to great or whether good is just going to be good enough. That's really the challenge and the art and science of coaching – recognizing what's there and making a few little adjustments or changes to make a player great, and better than everybody else. To take a player from number10 in the ranking to 1 at the pro level can be a huge achievement. Figuring it out, and deciding what you are going to do to make change, that's the essence of great, interpretative coaching. That's where coaching becomes so specialized and where experience starts playing a larger role. Making difficult concepts and situations easy and simple for players to understand is an important skill coaches have to possess, to create a winning environment.

Vidal: From a strategic and tactical perspective, how has the professional tour evolved since your playing days?

Rolley: The professional players today are outstanding athletes, better than ever. Equipment has increased the power and the skill level of many players. So today's game is a far more violent game than it used to be. With the speed increasing there is less finesse involved in today's game. For example, on the men's side, the serve is bigger and better than ever, the dominance of the forehand is a big factor, and players have to play well from every part of the court. Speed, power, reaction, balance, and endurance have become much bigger factors in pro tennis. The two-handed backhand has certainly revolutionized the game; we're seeing the slice come back as a variety. Nothing is untouched. You need every shot and the ability to do everything, placement, power, consistency, etc. to be a great player.

On the women's side, the serve has definitely upgraded to a higher level. You have to be able to serve well now to play good women's tennis. The speed, the power, certainly the two-handed backhand up the line and the big forehand have all evolved as huge weapons in today's game. You have big, strong athletes who are at the top of the game.

Vidal: Do you see the same amount of variety in the women's game as you've seen in the men's game?

Rolley: I see the effort to have it. However, with the speeds increasing, and the women hitting with less spin, there is less opportunity for a large variety of shots. The greater speed and depth of the ball provides less approach shot chances. You certainly see the women finishing at the net as well as strong groundstrokes, good movement, big forehands, and down-the-line backhands.

Vidal: Can you discuss the importance of playing instinctively as it relates to being a good thinker on the court?

Rolley: If you've learned and played the game properly in your early years and eliminated the things that you don't need, really focused on developing your game and stick with your top 3 or 4 patterns, then you're going to play instinctively and know what the right shot is. 70% of the time you're going to play one way and the other 30% you may do something different. That's where your instincts come in. It's like playing chess or playing cards. You've got to keep track of what's working and you need a pretty high level of consistency to have an accurate account.

Vidal: In terms of strategy and tactics, what are some of the key differences you've observed among the professional ranks vs. top collegiate and junior players?

Rolley: At the pro level, you have the good athlete, the consistency, the high level of speed and intensity. The pros move the ball extremely well around the court. An up-and-coming junior, on the other hand, may do a lot of these things well, just not well enough. A good junior, at about 14 years of age, has a pro game in mind – they look like little pros. They just need to continue to develop what they have and hopefully they'll be big enough, strong enough, and love the game enough to play at the pro level.

Your collegiate player often times can be limited but very good at a few things. When they're playing a pro who can counter what they do well, they simply won't win at that level.

Vidal: Besides more repetitions, what's your tactical advice for players with weaker backhands?

Rolley: First of all, define why the backhand is weak. Then try and fix it. You don't have to except it being a weakness if you are willing to make a change. Now, you don't have to have a real weapon on that side, but you certainly need a solid shot. In my mind, you start at the beginning with the fundamentals and find out where the problem is. Second, you must have a phenomenal forehand and great footwork to get around it, but this can also hinder improvements to the backhand. You're not going to be a great player if you have an apparent weakness.

In terms of patterns, if I have a weak backhand and we're both right-handed and I hit to your forehand, you're likely to hit it back crosscourt. Thus, learn to hit your backhand down-the-line so you end up getting into a forehand crosscourt pattern. You also need to just play in that corner (e.g., ad side for right-handers) and protect the backhand if it's not that solid. Again, if it's weak, it's going to get you in trouble. You've got to be able to keep your backhand deep and safe enough so that you don't get attacked.

Vidal: When competing against a pusher or counterpuncher, are there some general tactical guidelines that players should follow?

Rolley: Pusher has a negative connotation. Good pushers are people who are just really consistent, are annoying to play, and might drive you crazy during a match, since they get away with it, to a certain level. There are several tactics you can use by slicing the ball, playing short angle shots, or bringing them into the net. Instead of moving them side-to-side, which they tend to like, spend more time trying to move them forward and back. By putting them in a situation where they're forced to attack, you're likely to benefit from some errors.

No matter how you look at it, when facing someone whose personality is patient and consistent, you're in for an afternoon of work. Going into the match, you have to say to yourself, *"I have nothing to do all day so I'm going to fight all the way to the end and be as patient and as consistent as I can, but use the proper tactics to combat my opponent."*

Vidal: How do you coach your players to be great finishers, to close out sets and matches on a consistent basis?

Rolley: A great closer plays the way they've played throughout the match. Every point earned is just money in the bank, and you have to keep earning. So whether it's the first point of the match or the last point of the match, you've got to earn it. Nothing really should change in your game. Again, if certain patterns have been working, use them again to finish points off. I also think it's really important to practice a lot of tiebreakers, where every point is high stakes rather than wasting points in a game.

Generally speaking, for competitors at all levels, go with your best stuff and keep earning.

Vidal: What's your approach to scouting and how do you incorporate it into pre-match preparation?

Rolley: Scouting is an opportunity for me, as a coach, to look at the style and patterns of an opponent while playing. If I put myself in my player's shoes and play the points over in my mind, I could actually rehearse the shots that my player is going to need as preparation for the match. For example, I may say to my player, *"You realize your opponent has a very good slice backhand that angles short. What are you going to do with that ball?"* So you have to walk through those situations. The scouting process is basically a dress rehearsal.

Harold Solomon

Founder, Harold Solomon Tennis Institute

Inductee, International Jewish Sports Hall of Fame

ATP Career-High World Ranking #5 (1980)

Fort Lauderdale, Florida

"You have to be a problem solver on the court. The ability to do this is a huge key to being successful."

Vidal: How do you define high-percentage tennis?

Solomon: High percentage tennis looks differently for every player. A lot depends on style. When you think high-percentage tennis, you think margins (e.g., height over the net, hitting aggressively inside the lines, good shot selection based on court positioning, etc.). It's important that player's understand the attack zones, neutralizing zones, and the defensive zones of the court. The understanding of the court is the basis for playing high-percentage tennis.

In terms of style, what type of shots do you hit? Do you use more arc or do you play more like the professional women's players who hit the ball hard and flat? As an aside, the amount of errors in the women's game far outweighs those on the men's side because the men are able to track more balls down. The physicality (e.g., movement) on the women's side hasn't caught up with how hard and fast they're hitting the ball.

Vidal: From a strategic and tactical perspective, how has the professional tour evolved since your playing days?

Solomon: There are bunch of factors that come into play. First of all, today you have much better athletes. Guys are bigger, stronger, and faster. Also, racket technology and the strings have changed, although the technology in rackets hasn't had the same amount of impact of that in golf clubs today and how far golfers can drive the ball.

The training techniques such as the sophisticated work that's done on the track and inside the gym is another factor that is far superior to what we did in our generation. When I played, hardly any player was hitting with topspin or with a two-handed backhand; the courts were extremely fast, there were three grand slams on grass; indoor courts were like lightning, etc. The game has continued to change through phases, from the surfaces to the balls and so on.

Vidal: Can you discuss the importance of playing instinctively as it relates to being a good thinker on the court?

Solomon: Thinking is coming up with a strategy or tactic that's going to work against my opponent on the court. This may take place before the match or in the first couple games of the match, where I'm getting myself in a situation to effectively utilize my assets against my opponent's weaknesses to the best of my ability. Often, patterns come into play (e.g., the inside-out forehand into opponent's backhand side) and the the maturity of having trained yourself how to play where you're not out there mechanically thinking how you hit the ball and move. With experience, you become more aware of what's going on and anticipating probabilities. The better players are (almost) a shot ahead all of the time, always trying to put themselves in a more advantageous situation than your opponent. They may have one hundred options of where to hit the ball but because they've trained themselves properly, they'll choose the shot that is most appropriate in the moment. Thus, awareness and instinctiveness is generally born out of the work that gets done and the accumulation of the knowledge that you have.

You have to be a problem solver on the court, be able to do this (solve problems) quickly, rather than becoming the problem. The ability to do this is a huge key to being successful, particularly on the women's side where many of the players are their own biggest critic rather than their own biggest supporter on the court. It's a burden that's very detrimental to their ability to play consistently good tennis. You have a lot more ups and downs.

Vidal: As a coach that's had success working with players on both sides, how have you been able to turn that negative mindset around with your female students?

Solomon: It's a very difficult thing to turn around. There are lots and lots of conversations and trying to nip it in the bud. People, whether they recognize it or not, tend to do this (e.g., criticize oneself) when there is a payoff. It's about shifting the way that you think. The only way to make the shift is to catch yourself every single time that you that you have these thoughts that get in the way of your success. You're either going to go with it or not go with it. It's a choice and a very tough one at that.

Vidal: In terms of strategy and tactics, what are some of the key differences you've observed among the professional ranks vs. top collegiate and junior players?

Solomon: Once you get to the professional level, most players understand how to play high-percentage shots better than players at a lower level. Junior players feel like they have to change the direction of the ball on every shot; many juniors don't recognize that if you are locked into a backhand crosscourt rally with the opponent and your backhand is stronger, then that's a rally that's advantageous for you. The pros can lock in on a weakness and stay on it. Everybody wants to hit the ball hard these days. So as you get stronger, quicker, and gain more experience, it can often look like you're playing better tennis when you're actually not, even at the pro level. Because of the increase in power, it's also a lot harder to come to the net than it used to be. On the men's side, there's much more torque (and rotation on the ball) and the guys are hitting the ball so hard. Therefore, players tend to come in to the net less often. It's also important to realize that there have never been too many players with great volleys who use semi-western and western grips, another reason why we see less players looking to approach the net.

Vidal: Besides more repetitions, what's your tactical advice for players with weaker backhands?

Solomon: If the player is quick enough, you change the percentage of time the player spends on each side of the court. For example, you may go from a 50-50 split to a 75-25 (forehand-to-backhand) ratio. Players want to develop the ability to hit inside-out as well as inside-in forehands. Furthermore, rather than getting into backhand-to-backhand rallies, you want to hit your backhand up the line on occasion to improve the probabilities of your playing a forehand on the next shot.

If you can develop a really good slice backhand, you can cover up much of your weakness on the backhand side. The backhand slice is a shot that's really starting to come back. I was recently at the Australian Open watching the men play and guys were slicing the ball like crazy, not floating slices, but really going after it. At the end of the day, if your backhand isn't a good shot, you have to cover it up somehow.

Vidal: How much time should players invest on strengths development vs. improving weaknesses?

Solomon: It depends on the stage of your career (e.g., junior, collegiate, professional). We always work on trying to plug the holes while at the same time developing dominant shots. On the men's side, traditionally it's generally been the serve and the forehand.

On the women's side, it's been more backhand-oriented. There are a few professional women's players with strong serves such as Serena, although generally the women's serves have been weaker.

We're always looking to build weapons. If you look at top 5 men's touring professional David Ferrer (for example), he's smart, quick, fights like a dog, all great attributes. Speed is a huge weapon. Another weapon can be that you don't miss much. As a coach, you look at the physical makeup of a player and create a developmental plan where you build a game around two shots. You determine the tactics (e.g., slices, drop shots, approach shots, etc.) that will be involved in that style of game. A lot of it depends on the physicality and mentality of the player.

Most people focus attention on weaknesses and that's fine. You still have to practice strengths and build upon them all of the time. For players who have big shots, there's no reason those shots can't be getting bigger and bigger on a consistent basis.

Vidal: When competing against a pusher or counterpuncher, are there some general tactical guidelines that players should follow?

Solomon: Bringing people into the net is usually a good tactic. The ability to hit short angles slices and to drop shot are excellent shots. The most important thing is to not get impatient when you're playing counterpunchers. You must work the point and when you get the shot you like, go for it and do whatever you have to do (e.g., volley, swing volley, etc.) to finish off the point.

Many players get frustrated when playing against pushers. Realize that you often have to start the same point over again three or four times to win the point. They run everything down. Now, opening up the court with angles, especially against girls is particularly effective.

Another strategy and skill is pushing players back with heavy, deep balls, and looking for the opportunity to come in and knock off the return with swing volleys. For the most part however, players who are steady don't do well in the forecourt, so if you can figure out ways to bring them in, you'll do well by taking them out of their comfort zone.

Vidal: What needs to be done to bring more variety back into the women's game?

Solomon: I think it's starting to happen; where girls are hitting their forehands more like guys. They're getting stronger and are able to start brushing up on the ball more to create more spin. I think Henin started that when she changed her forehand.

Women's tennis always seems to follow the men, but it's like 10 years behind. Whether the serve will ever end up becoming a huge part in the women's game, I'm not so sure. The second serve is still the weakest part of women's games. It's the most vulnerable to attack.

We will continue to see bigger and stronger girls at the highest levels of the game. There's always exceptions, but it's very difficult for a girl (who's small of stature) to become top 5 in the world.

Vidal: How do you coach your players to be great finishers, to close out sets and matches on a consistent basis?

Solomon: It's a very difficult thing to teach a player to stay in the moment. The way I see it is that players get caught up in the soap opera of tennis instead of playing tennis. They start thinking "What if I beat this person or what if I lose, what people will think, etc." It's important to play one point at a time and stay in the moment tactically (e.g., what you've been doing that's successful) regarding what's going on, as opposed to focusing on the result or what will happen in defeat. Avoid thinking about outcomes and stay focused tactically in the present. That' the key to success.